1 MONTH OF
FREE
READING

at

www.ForgottenBooks.com

ISBN 978-0-260-00910-4
PIBN 10921898

n of Policy Is Toward Bilateral Agreements
B. K. Madan.

aspect of the central problem of commercial polic
immediate and urgent attention is that of reducir
ional trade. This end is sought to be attained in
d control of international trade is necessarily
which may be classified into three rather well
n of three distinct schools of thought in respect
government of trade between nations. The three
:hool of equality of treatment, usually known as
.icy, the school of special bargaining, which tries
by buying and selling concessions or special
by bilateral compacts, and the school of group or
; to get outlets for trade by joining with several
or multi-lateral compact for lower national barrie
lity practice, the special bargaining policy, and
represent the real thought and practice of the
ill of them the different nations struggle to reduc
with an eye to the opportunities of their own

the group or areal agreements, however, (illustrat
en Netherlands, Belgium and Luxembourg, by which
to reduce their tariffs as against each other, 10
years or 50 percent in all and offered the benefit;
ement to any other nation that cared to adhere)
tively free custom areas provides the most promisir
agh the present unpromising situation for internati

ost desirable line of development under the presen
nately not the most general direction in which
on and widespread, almost universal, form in which
towards planned or regulated trade is manifesting
iborate network of negotiated bilateral treaties
f rates, but quotas and other forms of quantita-
nmercial agreements and even financial provisions.
is a very careful balancing of concessions on
lculated exchanges of various kinds of goods again:

such treaties is so strictly circumscribed and
ons that their results must fall short of the free.
;, for many of the most sound and profitable tradi;
iered. Nevertheless, limited treaties of this kin
ing, the only way of overcoming the many barriers
empts at a 'broad solution by concerted action
ig failed to produce tangible results at the World
nc developments have received a distinct stimulus
each country has to flounder its own way through
tions as best as its circumstances and conditions

nd Problems Of International Trade"
B. K. Madan
nal of Economics -- April 1935

Practical Difficulties in the Way of More Foreign Trade
R. A. Goslin

"First of all, in order to restore our export trade to 1929 levels without at the same time lending money abroad, we would have to buy about $2,826,000,000 more goods from other countries than we bought in 1934. If we wanted to receive the same income from our foreign investments we would have to add another $524,000,000. And if we insisted on the repayment of our war debts, we would have to import even more. How would this affect the domestic market for American farm and industrial products? If our people bought imported goods, would they or could they also buy goods Made in U. S. A. ?

"It is claimed that the increased income from exports and from foreign investments would make it possible for our people to buy more imports and still spend the same amount of money for domestic goods. However, there is no doubt that some industries such as textiles, would be hard hit by foreign competition, and workers would be displaced.

"It has been estimated that out of 8,800,000 wage-earners employed in American factories and mills in 1929, 2,134,000 were engaged in industries whose products were protected by tariffs.

"There are powerful business groups who have a vested interest in maintaining high import duties and keeping out foreign competition. They descend on Congress as soon as they learn of any move to lower the tariff on articles they produce. They apply pressure to prevent such changes, and conduct an active propaganda campaign in favor of continued protection.

"Even if the tariff were lowered to admit more imports, the internationalists would have to face the difficulty of finding markets for our goods. Other countries have passed high tariffs and increased their own production. Not only the retreat to nationalism but also the setting up of more and more machinery has tended to lessen the opportunities for trade except in essential raw materials. The machine makes it possible for more and more countries to make the same goods with the same degree of skill and efficiency. This reduces the advantages of specialization.

"Again, if we decide on a policy of freer trade we must face the difficulties of greater and greater competition. Nations, like individuals, are operating under a competitive system. That system necessitates a struggle for control of raw materials, methods of transportation and available markets. Many times that struggle has become bitter and ruthless. There is little room for genuine cooperation. Business men do not help their competitors. The corporation of one country enters into keen competition with great combines of one or two other countries. And economic competition is more likely to make for war than peace.

"Whichever policy we choose, it would be necessary to place some or all of our producers under a certain amount of control. The government would have to exercise a guiding hand in making the necessary adjustments. If exports were not to be increased or were to be further decreased, strict government regulation of farm production would be necessary. If tariffs were lowered and international trade were revived, there would have to be some degree of control over domestic production so that imports could be admitted.

10797

"What are the chances of carrying out either program successfully in the United States? Americans don't like government control. It goes against the grain. We are used to wide open spaces of liberty. We were brought up to believe that private initiative is the mainspring of business enterprise."

"Made in U. S. A."
Ryllis Alexander Goslin
Headline Book No. 2
The Foreign Policy Association
1935

Latin American Trade Possibilities
Hon. Cordell Hull

"This raises a large question with respect to the policy which should be pursued in the Western Hemisphere. In Latin America, under the pressure of the gap in the balance of payments created by the fall in the price of their leading exports, an effort was first made to close this gap by allowing the exchanges to seek the level required to balance their international accounts. Subsequently, it was necessary to introduce the device of exchange control whereby the out-payments and in-payments were forcibly brought into accord. Since, at the official rate, there is not enough foreign exchange available in these countries to meet all payments, exporters have been compelled to wait frequently many months for payment in terms of dollars. In some cases, the United States might compel immediate payment by blocking the exchange created by American purchases of imports from these countries. By undertaking such clearing arrangements, however, the United States would encourage the spread of clearing and compensation agreements over the Western Hemisphere, thereby prolonging and strengthening the grip of these injurious practices upon international trade. If, on the other hand, this country takes a sympathetic position looking toward the gradual re-establishment of a free exchange market, and refuses to force upon these countries preferential treatment of our own nationals and trade, we shall hasten the movement toward liberal commercial policy and bring nearer the day when all these artificial restraints are wholly removed from international economic relations.

"Conditions are improving with sufficient rapidity in the Latin-American countries to make one optimistic that if right policies are pursued, the achievement of free exchange markets is feasible in the not far distant future. This is a time in which it is important to resist immediate and short-sighted advantage and to look toward the steady rebuilding of a sound international structure with a view to achieving the far more valuable long-run benefits obtained thereby."

"International Trade"
Honorable Cordell Hull - Secretary of State
Address - World Trade Dinner—Nov. 1, 1934.

Inherent National Advantages Still Allow Room For Trade
Henry A. Wallace

"The contention that it is useless now to press against the world tide and try for international trade is strengthened in some measure by the contention that machinery levels off regional potentialities; that the products of one civilized country soon become very much like those of another country; and that to trade like products is simply a waste of money and time. The drift toward economic nationalism is therefore bound to accelerate, according to this argument, as the years go by.

"Undoubtedly there is something to this argument. Imitative factories producing similar products can spring up in almost any soil and climate. That clustering of specialized skill which makes Detroit, for instance, a motor center may be bodily removed, in a manner of speaking, to China, through importations of machine tools and a few factory technicians. The increasing success of the Russians, never distinctly a machine-minded people, in turning out tractors and other modern equipment somewhat like our own, may also be cited as a case in point. But I think it is obvious that in a sane world, without barriers of hatred and suspicion, the Russians would have chosen to develop products more in line with their own national genius, and trade such products for our machines, rather than to turn out toilsome imitations on their own soil.

"Mechanization may tend to make the manufactured products of all countries more nearly alike; but the tendency cannot be considered apart from the question of raw materials; and the natural zones of the highest potential production in agriculture and mining are little subject to mechanistic change. There is a best place, and a second and third-best place in the world to mine coal or grow cotton, just as there are favored and less favored cotton and coal regions within the United States. We cramp the finest possibilities of a civilization when, blinded by local pride, either regional or national, we blink at plain facts.

"The same thing holds true of innate or inherited capacities. England makes better cloth than we do, and better hand-made shoes. France, I am told, makes better wine. Unquestionably, however, we raise apples more cheaply than France. Accordingly, one of our first approaches toward dealing with the world again, on a new basis, is as simple and sensible as a swap between two pioneer farm neighbors. We traded France some of our apples for some of its wine.

"International trade is not necessarily complicated. If we allow ourselves again to approach world trading as if it were a sacred and impenetrable mystery, then we are likely again to get into another jam. The considerations which make international business desirable are plain. Recently I heard for the first time a saying popular in Arkansas. It was that Arkansas could build a wall a mile high around its borders and go right on living and doing business. That may be true; but I doubt if even the noisiest orator in Arkansas would claim that the people there could live as well or as spaciously as they do even now, exchanging goods and services with the people of other states. It is equally obvious that we take only meager advantage of this opportunity to exchange special products or special capacities if we coop up the process within national boundaries.

10797

in respect to raw materials and handicraft products,
s desirable now as it ever was; and I deny that
tional differences in skill and ingenuity. Where
 the result is impermanent. Chinese to whom we
a out a good Ford car, but the next improvement
inery which makes it, would be likely to occur
   On the contrary, we could train American workmen
 them with the best Chinese devices, yet the best
till come from China. Granting then a certain
nt to standardize and level the product, there .
a great variety of inherent national advantages
borly world, would allow plenty of room for trade."

   "America Must Choose"
   Henry A. Wallace

at The Internationalists Say
   Ryllis A. Goslin

arguments for high tariff and isolation, let's
lists say about the advantages of foreign trade.

i Nations are Dependent on Each Other"

 the people of a town or village could supply their
 ase their own food, weave their own clothes out of
 thered, build their own houses out of the lumber
  their children at the village school. But the days
 and wood stoves are gone. Science and technology
 of labor, whereby each man or community or nation
 l work of production. This makes each one more and
 :.

Increases Wealth"

 increased the wealth of a community or a nation.
 vide up the work to be done, they developed greater
 r on, communities specialized in the production
 changed them for those of other communities. As
 people could produce more and therefore had more
 trade gives every individual, community, and
 ze in the production of those goods which he or
 luce.

 economic suicide for us to require every community
 ies to produce all it needs, since it would deprive
 a division of labor. In the same way, it would
 ofitable interchange of goods among nations. Be-
 natural resources, the aptitudes of its people or
 y is able to produce certain goods more cheaply and
 ts wealth will increase as it specializes in these
 r those which other countries can produce to better
 es excels in the production of cotton, tobacco,
 riety of manufactured articles which can be turned

out cheaply by machine in great quantities with little labor. Tropical countries
in turn have the advantage over us in the production of coffee, tea, rubber and
certain fruits. England has become famous for her woolen goods, France for
her wine, Japan for her silk, Holland for her lace, and China for her embroider-
ies.

"3. "Trade Raises the Standard of Living"

"The exchange of goods enables each country to confine its efforts to
producing goods which it is best fitted to produce, either because of natural
resources or special skill. In this way it can produce more, and thus have
more to exchange for other goods. The internationalists claim that greater
production results in higher wages which can be used to purchase more and more
imported commodities. And thus the entire standard of living is raised. High
wages in the United States are not the result of the tariff, but of our great
wealth of resources and our superior methods of production. The American working
man gets a higher wage than his foreign rival primarily because he is able to
produce more with the help of abundant resources and better technique.

"On the other hand, when men or nations try to produce things they are
less fitted to do, they become less productive. This means lower wages, less
goods, and a lower standard of living.

"4. "Culture and Progress Follow Trade"

"It is said that civilization has followed the path of commerce. The
traders of ancient times transferred knowledge, skill and invention from one
city to another as they carried their goods. Cities grew up and flourished
as centers of trade--Tyre and Sidon, Antioch, Carthage, Pisa, Athens, Rome.
Today trade makes possible the rapid communication of technical, scientific
and artistic advances from one country to another.

"5. "Freer Trade Would Promote World Peace"

"The isolationists claim that the United States would run less risk
of being involved in war if it kept its trade at home. In reply, the internationalists say that, although isolation might be a temporary solution for us
in the immediate future, isolation would not be a wise or practical policy for
any nation in the long run. Almost no other country except Russia could hope
to live on its own resources. Countries like Switzerland, Czechoslovakia, or
Belgium could not possibly shut themselves off from outside markets without
changing their whole way of life.

"Furthermore, they say, trade in itself is not a serious cause of war.
The race for colonies and the struggle for markets and raw materials tend to
become bitter when nations close their home markets by raising high tariff
walls. We can already see some of the results of the attempts at nationalism
in various parts of the world. Japan, poor in natural resources and overpop-
ulated, has seized a large part of China. Italy, in need of raw materials and
markets, is trying to take possession of Ethiopia. Germany's extreme nationalism under Hitler has increased the fear of war in Europe.

"Only by exchanging goods peacefully, the internationalists say, can
we hope to avoid imperialism and conflict. Gradually then we can develop a

f cooperation whereby all can have the advantages of a division of
d access to the necessary raw materials."

"Made in U. S. A."
Ryllis Alexander Goslin
Headline Book No. 2
The Foreign Policy Association 1935

What the Economic Nationalists Say
Ryllis A. Goslin

"1. "Be Economically Independent"

As the richest country in the world, we have plenty of land and nearly
resources and raw materials needed for our productive plant. We have
ce of becoming more nearly self-sufficient than any other nation. We
herefore, be doing the world as well as ourselves a service if we put
house in order and ceased to depend for our livelihood or our prosperity
eeds and desires of the rest of the world. Economic nationalism, say
nders, is not a selfish or narrow policy. Rather, it grows out of a
dmirable desire to be able to take care of one's own needs instead of
pendent on others.

"2. "Avoid the Uncertainty of Foreign Markets"

It is hard to depend on selling goods abroad. Foreign nations are
t any moment to raise tariffs, or decide to accept only so much goods,
cut us off from an important source of income. Our factories and
come dependent on the purchasing power of people in other nations and
e may suffer from their depressions. Or foreign producers may suddenly
ge quantities of goods on our shores at low prices and ruin our home
es.

If we kept our trade at home, we could study the home market, know
to produce, and how much we could sell. But foreign trade is always
n. Why not, therefore, pay more attention to the home market and stop
about the economic troubles of other countries?

"3. "Big Foreign Markets Are Gone"

We have gotten into the habit of thinking that by dint of effort, we
scover greater and greater foreign markets for our goods. But the
ists say we must face the facts. The reason why our exports were
during the war was not because of American initiative and enterprise,
use Europe was at war. They did not have time to cultivate lands,
crops, and manufacture goods. But when the war was over, their men
< to work again. They not only produced as much as before, they produced
hey too had the advantages of scientific methods and power machinery.
t expect to sell goods to people who now produce their own. Science,
y, and the desire of nations to be economically independent have cut
chance to sell our goods abroad.

"4. "Foreign Trade is Not Important Anyway"

"Our foreign trade is actually a very small part of our total business. Our total production in 1929 was 52 billion dollars worth of goods.
Our total exports in that year amounted to just over 5 billion dollars, or
about 10%. In 1931 our exports had dropped to about 7½% of our total
production. Export trade accounted for only about 4 dollars out of every 100
dollars of income. It is far more important, the nationalists say, for us
to remember that 90% of our total market has always been at home and try,
therefore, to restore the purchasing power of our own people.

"5. "Protect the American Standard of Living"

"If we are to restore the purchasing power of our people and protect the American standard of living, we must protect our industry and our
agriculture with a high tariff. Other countries can often produce goods
more cheaply because of lower living standards. In order to meet such
competition American producers would have to lower prices and reduce wages,
and this in turn would cut the purchasing power and the standard of living.

"6. "We Must be Prepared in Case of War"

"Again, the economic nationalists urge us to protect and strengthen
our own industries, so that we would be able to furnish our own supplies in
time of war. They warn us that it is dangerous to be dependent on other
nations for raw materials, and advise us to encourage home production and
to discover substitutes wherever possible for the necessary raw materials."

"Made in U. S. A."
Ryllis Alexander Goslin
Headline Book No. 2
The Foreign Policy Association 1935

Planned Economy and Laissez-faire Economy: Walter Lippman

"And so it may be said, perhaps, that the difficulty of a self-
sufficient controlled economy would lie in the lack of wisdom for centralized
direction and the necessity for regimentation; that the difficulty of international laissez-faire has been found to lie in the immense human resistance
which has developed to the consequences of free competition.

"Therefore, one must conclude, I should think, that profound readjustments of capital and labor will be called for quite regardless of whether one
prefers an open or a closed economy. I strongly suspect that the amount of
planning, of centralized control, and of regimentation which we adopt will be
determined by the amount of readjustment which circumstances force upon us.

"For the American economy is obviously not now organized for a policy
of self-containment. Very important producing interests both in agriculture
and in industry are adapted to world markets, and must face enormous losses
and human misery if those markets are permanently lost. Those who argue that
the exports of the United States are a negligible fraction of the total
production are using statistics to obscure the realities. To reduce American
10797

agriculture to a self-contained market would, it is estimated, call for reducing the productive acreage by 40,000,000 acres of average land or by 60--70,000,000 acres of poor land. This is not a negligible readjustment. What would be required, in the way of loss of capital and displacement of labor in order to reduce American industry to a basis of self-sufficiency, I do not know, though it was estimated in 1928 that two and a half million families were dependent upon industrial production for export.

"So, if at this moment in the autumn of 1933, I had to testify in answer to the question: Is the United States passing through a social revolution which will bring into being a closed and controlled economy?, I should have to answer in some such way as this: The economy of the United States is dislocated. Since the economic relationships which existed before 1929 cannot for various reasons be restored, 'recovery' involves certain deep readjustments. The system of free enterprise has become too rigid and the sense of social obligations too acute to permit the carrying out of these readjustments by individual action and individual sacrifice. Therefore, by the logic of the circumstances, the United States has been driven to experiment in collective control designed to facilitate the necessary readjustments. These experiments have their roots in the desire for recovery rather than in a popular enthusiasm for the ideal of an authoritarian state and a planned economy. They are, therefore, practical expedients rather than revolutionary processes. But it is possible that the dislocation may not yield to the expedients, thus compelling resort to more drastic ones. It is possible that the expedients may themselves deepen the dislocation by inhibiting the free enterprise upon which an essential part of recovery depends. It is possible that the expedients will seem admirable and equally possible that they will seem detestable.

"And therefore the only conclusion that is now justified, it seems to me, is that as long as the expression of opinion remains free, it will be immediate experience rather than theory which will dictate the course of policy. Indeed, the more I reflect upon the problem, the better I understand why revolutionists bent upon a radical transformation of human society do, and in fact must, begin by abolishing freedom of expression. There is no other way in which a complete transition can be effected swiftly except by preventing the people from impeding, deflecting, and limiting the change in accordance with their experience."

"Self-Sufficiency"
Walter Lippman
Foreign Affairs -- January 1934

Nationalism and Internationalism: Each Has Qualities of the Other:
Report of Economic Commission

"Economic nationalism, as the word is used today, means a policy of withdrawing from intercourse with foreign people to the greatest possible degree, a policy directed toward as much self-containment as is feasible in the modern world. It assumes that foreign commerce is dangerous because through it the economic disturbances arising in one country may be transmitted to another. It is based on the belief that the national security obtained by withdrawing from international commerce is worth the sacrifices that admittedly have to be made in the way of some depression of the standard of living unpredictable in degree, and of some narrowing of the national culture.

10797

"Internationalism when applied to economic matters means, on the contrary, intercourse between nations on a basis as free as possible from artificial barriers. It assumes that, since in the past one hundred years or more man reached his highest economic and cultural development while engaging in international trade and financial intercourse under minimum restrictions, to interrupt such intercourse would lead to a prolonged and profound economic dislocation everywhere and start mankind upon a road leading no one knows whither.

"Despite this apparently sharp contrast between these two philosophies, the Commission came to realize, as it proceeded with its inquiry, that in fact the distinction between them is superficial and unreal. No national policy is wholly nationalistic, none wholly internationalistic. Every policy contains many compromises; each is national in the sense that it is intended to promote the interests of the nation that adopts it. Internationalism is national in the sense that it is never in practice followed except with the intent to promote the interests of the nation. Internationalism in this sense is nationalistic. No one can say, except arbitrarily, at what point a given policy censes to be international and becomes national."

Report of Economic Commission
International Economic Relations. (Reprints Obtainable)
Published by University of Minnesota Press, Minneapolis, Minn., 1934

Steps Leading To Neutrality Act: W. W. Van Kirk

"Meanwhile, the trend toward war became more pronounced. Germany had thrown the Versailles Treaty overboard; tension points throughout Europe were increasing; Japan and China were at odds and the Far East was in turmoil; Italy was threatening to make war upon Ethiopia. The American people began asking the question: "If war comes, how can the United States keep out?".

"About this time a public debate was started regarding neutrality. Mr. Charles Warren who had been from 1914 to 1927 Assistant Attorney General in charge of enforcing the neutrality policies of the United States began the debate. Mr. Warren, while skeptical of the possibility of the United States maintaining strict neutrality, in the event of a major war, outlined a set of proposals which might help keep the United States out of war. These proposals were:

"1. All high-powered radio stations should be controlled and their use prohibited by all ships in our ports and waters, and, probably the transmission of secret code messages, even by foreign diplomats prohibited.

"6. The entrance of submarines into our ports or waters should be prohibited.

"7. Neither military nor commercial planes belonging to a belligerent should be allowed to descend on or pass over our territory.

"8. Merchant ships should be treated as adjuncts of navies and those of belligerent nations should be interned if they remain in neutral waters beyond a given time.

"9. Loans by private citizens to belligerent governments should be prohibited.

"10. American citizens should be prohibited from enlisting in belligerent armies.

"11. We must forego our so-called 'neutral rights' of trade and be content with what opportunities belligerents are willing to grant us.

"12. Assembling here and dispatch abroad by foreign officials of reserve members of belligerent armies or navies should be prohibited and possibly also American citizens forbidden to enlist abroad in belligerent forces.

"Things now moved swiftly. The Munitions Investigating Committee laid bare the story of America's participation in the World War. The facts unearthed by this investigation shocked the people. One of the most startling pieces of evidence unearthed by the Senate Committee was the confidential message cabled to President Wilson in March, 1917, by the American Ambassador to Great Britain. This message said in part, 'Perhaps our going to war is the only way in which our present preeminent trade position can be maintained and a panic averted. The submarine has added the last item to the danger of uncertainty about our being drawn into the war, no more considerable credit can be privately placed in the United States and a collapse may come in the meantime.'

"It became increasingly clear to the American people that if the United States were to be kept out of another war steps would have to be taken to regulate our trade with warring nations. A group of Congressmen and Senators drew up a set of recommendations forbidding the shipment of all arms and munitions to any warring nations; prohibiting American bankers from making loans or extending credit to a warring nation; compelling American exporters to ship at their own risk any article declared to be contraband by any belligerent, denying passports to American citizens travelling in war zones.

"A vigorous discussion followed the publication of these proposals. The upshot of the whole matter was the adoption by the American Congress in late August, 1935, of a Neutrality Act."

"The A B C of American Neutrality"
Walter W. Van Kirk
Federal Council of the Churches of Christ in America - 1935

10797

Problems Of Neutrality: Charles Warren

"Neutrality is difficult to preserve, except in case of a war between small nations or one in which our commercial interests are not gravely affected. If a war should fail to remain localized and should extend so as to involve other major powers, then the complications likely to arise, the belligerent propaganda inspired in this country, the oratory in Congress, the pressure from commercial and financial interests affected by actions of the belligerents, might easily lead us to the verge of war.

"Under such conditions neutrality and adherence to peace would be difficult. Americans must be willing to pay a price for it--a price which would most certainly touch their pocketbooks and their pride.

"In an article in April, 1934, entitled 'Troubles of a Neutral,' I pointed out that sacrifices of alleged rights must be made and obligations must be assumed by our citizens as a part of that price. From observations of actual difficulties in the path of a neutral, made by me when as Assistant Attorney General of the United States I had charge of all matters relating to the war and neutrality which came to the Department of Justice from 1914 to 1917, I suggested, on the basis of this experience, twelve subjects as to which laws should be enacted in the effort to avoid the frictions, complications and dangers which the United States actually encountered as a neutral during the World War.

"Of these twelve subjects, five have been taken care of in the Neutrality Act of Aug. 31, 1935--embargo on 'arms, munitions, or implements of war'; prohibition of shipment of such articles in American ships; prohibition of travel by an American citizen on a ship of a belligerent nation except at his own risk; regulation of belligerent submarines in our ports and waters; and further restrictions on ships attempting to supply belligerent war vessels from our ports.

"There remain, however, at least three major subjects as to which no legislative enactment has been made or legislative policy declared, and which urgently demand attention. The first of these is the question of armed merchantmen of a belligerent.

"Under international law, a neutral nation is obliged to use due diligence to prevent the equipping and departure from its ports of any belligerent vessel which it has reasonable ground to believe is intended to cruise or carry on war against a power with which the neutral is at peace. At the same time, under international law, a merchantman of a belligerent is allowed to carry armament for defensive purposes without taking on the character of a war vessel.

"During the World War the United States found great difficulty in making the decision whether armed belligerent merchantmen in its ports were armed for defense or offense. . . . . .

"Hence, having full power by domestic legislation to regulate in its own ports the presence or operation of any foreign vessel, this country should by statue now exclude from its ports in time of war all armed merchantmen of a belligerent or treat them as ships of war. Such action was taken by Holland during the World War.

10797

"The second subject which undoubtedly will require action by Congress
is that of loans and credits to the belligerent nations or to their citizens.

"But public loans to a belligerent government nowadays form but a small
part of the financial assistance which may be rendered by a neutral to further
the war. Commercial loans and credits, whether made to a government or to its
citizens, constitute the bulk of the financing for the belligerents in a
neutral country. These latter must also be prohibited or restricted.

"That such legislation will result in considerable loss of business to
our citizens is one of the prices which they must pay to remain at peace. At
the same time, it should be noted that the present statute imposing an embargo
on arms and munitions will itself, ipso facto, result in the restriction of commercial loans and credits to a belligerent; for hitherto such financing has been
largely for the purchase of arms and munitions.

"The third subject to which our government, for the maintenance of
neutrality, must give careful consideration is that of contraband.

"Hence the question arises: What can the United States do with reference
to its contested right of trade, now or at the outset of another serious war?

"In the first place, American citizens should consider carefully the
reason given by the belligerents for their extension of the term 'contraband,'
namely, that, under modern conditions, the success of a war depends not only on
troops but on the commerce and labor of the civil population; and that supplies
to the army and navy and to the civil population are of almost equal importance
in their effect upon the outcome of a war.

"From the belligerent's standpoint, neutral shipments of food, chemicals,
metals, rubber, and other contraband articles to an enemy give military aid to
the enemy equally with neutral shipments of arms and munitions. Americans,
therefore, should ask themselves the question: Why, logically, should a neutral
not adopt toward these other forms of contraband, which are of importance to a
belligerent in waging war, the same attitude as toward arms and munitions?

"There are four different policies which the United States might adopt
with reference to this contraband question.

"The more reasonable and the least complicated policy would be to give
formal notice, by Congressional action or by Presidential proclamation, that all
sales and exports of articles declared contraband by any belligerent are to be at
the risk of the seller or exporter, and that our government during the war will
not enter into controversy with the belligerents, but that after the war it will
assert claims before some international tribunal for damages in behalf of such
persons, based on any right of trade found to exist under international law.

"Any one of these courses might call for considerable sacrifice of
American trade, and unquestionably loud and passionate outcry would arise from
cotton, wheat, meat, copper, steel and other agricultural and commercial interests
affected.

10797

"But the issue is a simple one. Should the United States insist on disputed rights of trade in contraband and run the risk of war in order to protect the profits to be made out of war by some of its citizens? Is the right of a citizen to trade in contraband to be regarded as superior to the right of the nation to preserve itself from the risk of war?

"A vigorous address was made on these questions by Admiral William S. Sims (retired) on May 8, 1935, in which he said: 'The point of the whole business is this--we cannot keep out of war and at the same time enforce the freedom of the seas, that is, the freedom to make profits out of countries in a death struggle. If a war arises, we must, therefore, choose between two courses--between great profits with grave risks of war on the one hand or smaller profits and less risk on the other.

"'The time to decide is now, while we can think calmly and clearly, before war propaganda gets in its deadly work. * * * Therefore, let every citizen who has the cause of honorable peace at heart take this stand: 'Our trade as a neutral must be at the risk of the traders; our army and navy must not be used to protect this trade. It is a choice of profits or peace. Our country must remain at peace'.'

"But the most ardent advocates of neutrality must be made to realize, furthermore, that even with all the legislation already enacted or still proposed, and even with this Presidential action, the United States cannot be certain of keeping out of war. For one of the chief sources of danger to our neutrality still remains untouched. It was the unrestricted submarine warfare of the Central Powers which actually brought the United States into the conflict; and up to date there has been no international agreement regulating the future use of submarines.

"Moreover, a new element presenting a possible danger to neutral lives and neutral trade has arisen in the probable use of airplanes for bombing merchant vessels which refuse to comply with belligerent orders. Therefore, there still remains the danger from these sources to the lives of American passengers or crews on American ships--especially passengers and crews who are not engaging in transactions with belligerents. And in spite of all legislation now enacted or proposed such loss of life in the future would probably again arouse our people to war.

"When, therefore, everything is said that can be said for a policy of strongly entrenched neutrality (with which I am in full sympathy), it still remains true that the United States can best keep out of war by a policy of hearty and positive cooperation with other nations in attempting to prevent the occurence of wars."

"Pitfalls In The Path of Neutrality"
Charles Warren
The New York Times Magazine
October 20, 1935

10797

ls And Neutrality Policy: W. W. Van Kirk

ons Control Board met in late September.   It drew up
h might fairly be regarded as 'munitions and imple-
oosevelt, on September 25, made public a list of the
he Neutrality Law. These implements include rifles,
ombs, torpedos, tanks, armored trains, vessels of
designed peculiarly for military purposes, aircraft
me-throwers.

policy has as yet been made regarding what, if any, raw
d in the embargo list in the event of war. The ques-
nitions Control Board must ask are these: What are
. raw materials as cotton, copper and other 'border-
ded as 'implements of war'? Under a strict interpre-
t is the exportation of these 'borderline' materials to
of war? No official of the national administration has,
tions. And yet it is precisely these questions that
statesmen. If, for example, the League were to im-
inst a nation resorting to war, would or would not the
shipment of essential raw materials to the so-called

e A B C of American Neutrality"
   By Walter W. Van Kirk
bl.--Federal Council of The Churches
     of Christ in America

For Neutrality: Editorial Wallace's Farmer

ether he wants the United States to get into another
 and his answer is 'No.'

d the same question of any American at the time of the
ave given the same answer. Yet we got into the War of

e same question in 1914, the answer would have been
the latest world war, in 1917.

hen we claimed we wanted to stay out?

on in each case was that we got to hunting profits from
 we got into war without knowing it.

f goods we had to sell. We found that selling these
had to protect our merchant ships from the blockading
war. In trying to protect this trade, we got into
in 1812, with Germany in 1917.

"When we try to make money out of a world war, we get into it ourselves. . .

"Munitions makers were making money. But so, apparently, were wheat, hog and cotton farmers. Prices were up. Things were booming.

"Actually, how much was being made? We shipped abroad all sorts of goods. What did we get in exchange? Nothing, except cancellation of our debts to Europe and pieces of paper signed by European nations, saying they would pay us some day. . . .

"To protect these (private) loans, to protect these apparently profitable exports, we tried to keep British ships from blocking trade, and we tried to prevent German submarines from sinking merchant ships. Finally, after quarreling with both sides, we went to war with Germany.

"That war cost us $25,000,000,000 in direct costs. Our unpaid war loans come to $12,000,000,000 more. Interest charges on these debts, care of wounded veterans and similar expenses run the total up to $55,000,000,000 and the end is not yet. Worse than this, we dislocated our industry and agriculture so that the war prepared the ground for the depression of 1929. Farmers plowed up pastures and increased wheat, hog and cotton production for a temporary foreign market.

"With this experience in mind, how can we stay out of the next war if it comes? We need to remember that it costs money to stay out of war. We'll have to pay for neutrality. We will be tempted with the offers of high prices for wheat, cotton and pork if we overproduce again and guarantee delivery across the water. Yet those high prices will be mostly fakes. We'll be offered I.O.U.'s again, and we should know now how much those are worth.

"In return for these fake profits, we'll run the certainty of getting into war. We can avoid it by forbidding loans to warring nations, by blocking shipments of munitions, and--most important--by insisting that shipments to warring nations be made at the risk of those hungry for profits. If submarines sink the ships, that's their hard luck.

"If we stay neutral, we must pay the cost of neutrality. We must be willing to go without speculative war-time prices for wheat, hogs and cotton. But in the end, it will cost us a lot less, in money as well as in lives, to wage neutrality instead of waging war."

"It Costs Money to Stay Out of War"
Editorial
Wallace's Farmer and Iowa Homestead
October 12, 1935

Isolation to Prevent War: Ryllis Alexander Goslin

"But there is another important group of people who believe strongly that we should keep our trade and business interests at home for somewhat different reasons. They see very clearly the difficulties of trade that have already been pointed out--the uncertainty of world markets, increasing competition, and growing nationalism in Europe and Asia. They see also the dangers of imperialism and war.

"Therefore, they advise us to isolate ourselves as far as possible from the rest of the world not as a defense in case of war, but as a method of avoiding war. If we were not interested in securing foreign markets, our merchants would not be entering into keen competition with the merchants of other nations. We would not have to build up our Navy to protect our trade, our investments, or the property of our citizens abroad. The large profits of war trade would cease to interest us. These isolationists believe that, if we could work out plans to supply the needs of our own people, we would then be in a better position to enter into a program of real cooperation with the other nations of the world."

> "Made in U. S. A."
> Ryllis Alexander Goslin
> Headline Book No. 2
> The Foreign Policy Association
> 1935

How Far United States Can Go In Joint Action Without Becoming Involved:
Shepardson and Scroggs

"To many American citizens it has always seemed that the foreign policy of the United States rested, and should rest, upon two basic principles: to uphold the Monroe Doctrine, and to avoid foreign entanglements. In the popular mind this means, in effect, that Europe must keep out of the affairs of the New World, and that the United States must keep out of the affairs of Europe. The general lay idea of neutrality seems to conform to these broad conceptions of foreign policy; it means little more than keeping out of war. These prevailing concepts, however, do not per se spell isolation; they are not a bar to international cooperation, if this cooperation does not lead to 'involvement'. Then arises the practical question, How far does the United States feel that it can go in joint action with other powers without danger of becoming involved? What contribution might it naturally be expected to make to the advancement of collective security?

"In the spring of 1935 Professor Jessup of Columbia University attempted to answer these questions. It was his conclusion, based on a careful study of the record, that the United States stood ready to join in international agreements (1) for the limitation of land, sea, and air armaments; (2) for the regulation of the traffic in arms; and (3) for redetermining and clarifying the rights and duties of neutrals in time of war. Furthermore, on the express condition that the powers should agree upon a general program of disarmament, the United States was prepared to conclude additional agreements, including: (1) pacts of non-aggression, carrying the pledge to move no armed forces across frontiers; (2) pacts of consultation, provided that they embodied no advance commitment regarding actions to be taken as a result of consultation; and (3) an undertaking to renounce the exercise of so-called neutral rights in dealing with aggression, if the United States concurred independently in the identification of the aggressor.

"On the negative side there were certain obligations which the record showed that the United States government was not ready to assume. For example, it would not engage in advance to participate in the application of sanctions or to use its

10797

military power for the enforcement of treaties; it would not give pledges in advance to accept the final decision of any international group or organization regarding its obligations. Nor would it fully renounce its rights as a neutral.

"This survey of the possible contribution of the United States to collective security, published in May, 1935, was both realistic and conservative. It seemed to hold out no false hopes whatsoever. Yet in the short space of three more months the immediate likelihood of even such limited contributions faded out; for toward the end of the session the mood of Congress, clearly in response to the public desire to keep aloof from troubles overseas, had become increasingly isolationist. Its members for the time being were not interested in plans for consultative pacts and arms limitation: they were interested in neutrality, because neutrality meant keeping out of war."

> The United States in World Affairs
> W. H. Shepardson and W. O. Scroggs
> Council on Foreign Relations
> Harper & Brothers, 1935.

Economic Policies Must Recognize Political Conditions: A. H. Hansen

"In the consideration of economic policies due regard must be given to political considerations. Economic policies that take no cognizance of political sensibilities are likely to endanger world stability and world peace. In the adoption of a tariff policy, for example, account should be taken not only of the effect on the domestic economy but also upon possible serious international complications. Tariff acts at times have had not only unfortunate economic consequences but have served to strengthen the hands of the aggressive militaristic party in foreign countries. The intense economic nationalism of the current depression finding expression in numerous arbitrary trade restrictions, monetary depreciation, and the like, has given rise to an immense amount of resentment and international ill-will.

"On the other hand no government can afford to take a strictly international viewpoint even though such a policy were, abstractly considered, wholly in the national interest; for, unless nationalistic sentiments or prejudices are mollified, dangerous consequences to the peace of the world may ensue. There is danger that a program of planned economic internationalism, such as that foreshadowed by the League of Nations and the various international economic conferences of the post-war period, may, in a highly nationalistic world, attempt too much and thereby destroy the very stability it is sought to achieve.

"Political and economic instability are intimately intertwined in a cause and effect relationship. Disarmament, regulation and control of the munitions industries, the World Court and other international institutions facilitating consultation and settlement of disputes — these are problems that concern international economic relations no less vitally than trade agreements, stable exchanges, and foreign lending.

"The treaty recently concluded with Cuba abolishes the former contractual right to intervene in Cuba and to participate in the determination of domestic policies such as those relating to finance and sanitation. The consummation of

10797

...stered by an international tribunal. However, until
. an international court, the problems must be dealt w
.nnels.

'national organizations, preferably non-political and .
.have been de**vi**sed to insure fair treatment and protec
.of such semi-governmental organizations as the Foreig.
'ritain and the newly formed Foreign Bondholders Prote.
.y."

.nsiderations With Respect to National Policy"
.nsen
.tional Economic Relations (Reprints Obtainable)
.ity of Minnesota Press

.al With The Cause of War: James P. Pope

.tes is now trying to establish such regulations in th.
.tions traffic, taking the profits out of war, and str
.vent our being drawn into a foreign war. * * * * .

. measures and I am supporting all of them. But, like
.e regulations, none of them go to the heart of the pr.
.ind and remove the cause of the plague. None of them
.venting war. The old saying that an ounce of preven.
.re is just as true in the matter of war as it is in

.war are economic conflicts brought on by currency dep.
. dislocated gold supplies, and there are racial and
. traditional rivalries, and armament races. The grea.
.h these underlying causes of war."

   "How We Can Stay Out of War"
   Hon. James P. Pope
   Radio Address - May 15, 1935

We Need Substitutes For War: Nicholas Murray Butler

"War is made not by peoples but by governments. It is the plain business of public opinion to control government so that it be not permitted to engage in international war and then, when hostilities are begun, to make emotional appeal to the men and women who must risk their lives and all that they own in order to take part in the conflict not of their own making and to carry it on under governmental direction. If public opinion tells governments that there shall be no war, there will be no war. If public opinion does not tell governments in unmistakable terms that there shall be no war, then there may be war.

"In order to prevent war, no farther formal action by any honorable government is necessary except to keep its plighted faith. Substantially every nation has united in the solemn declaration of the Pact of Paris, now some seven years old, to renounce war as an instrument of national policy. If this declaration be adhered to, if the plighted word of these governments be kept, what more is necessary, what new conferences, what additional agreements, are either possible or excusable?

"It is quite idle to say that the Pact of Paris does not relate to defensive war if by that be meant attack on another people in the name of self-defense. That is pure hypocrisy, for there can be no such defensive war if the Pact of Paris be adhered to. That nation which by armed force first attacks another in the guise of self-defense is waging not a defensive but an offensive war, and it has violated the Pact of Paris.

"What should follow the Pact of Paris? My answer is, those steps toward closer international understanding, toward fuller international cooperation, toward better world organization to deal with all those things which are common to civilized peoples everywhere. This means that the separate nations are to be constituted a genuine family and not merely a nominal one. They are to sit down together in constant council to deal with their common problems, to promote agriculture and industry, to relieve suffering, to raise the standard of living and to multiply the satisfactions and the happiness of men through the guaranty and the habit of that security and peace upon which these alone can rest. The one and only sure way to avoid war and to let militarism die of atrophy is to bring into existence effective and practical substitutes for war, and to insist that these substitutes for war be appealed to and used whenever international differences threaten. This means constant and intimate international consultation at Geneva, habitual use of the Permanent Court of International Justice at The Hague and the bringing into existence of an international police force to preserve world order and to control world traffic when there is need. Is that vision quixotic? Is that hope impracticable? If it be so, then man is not sufficiently civilized to protect his civilization and the tragedy, which our blindness for the moment may conceal, awaits either us or our children with appalling certainty. We shall have shown ourselves unable, through lack of insight, lack of courage and lack of capacity to preserve and to hand on to our children and our children's children that civilization which our fathers handed on to us. Now is the appointed time, now is the hour for public opinion to act and to insist that governments take their orders from it and from it alone, and that those orders be to protect and establish the peace of the world."

"On International Peace"
Nicholas Murray Butler
Broadcast - "The Family of Nations"
Nov. 11, 1934 - Vital Speeches

10797

ed Common Action: D. C. Blaisdell

ion of international problems is common action.
ustry and finance have been geared into an inter-
 American people, through artificial restrictions or
e, wish to experience a gradually declining standard
me expose themselves to the consequent international
tional course through the League and the World Court
. This simply means that the nations of the world
d by radio, by ships of commerce, by credits, by irc
 well as by music, art and literature, will take com
 interests are not destroyed by another world war.
a major war in Ethiopia, China or Central Europe mi
or wheat, hogs and cotton. But we also know that
 be impoverished and our farm prices would again col
serve our trade we might well again be drawn into
itable resulting post-war depression."

mer's Stake In World Peace"
C. Blaisdell
e Endowment for International Peace
, 1935.

ormed And Thinking Public: C. C. Davis

illustration of lop-sidedness and unbalance. I hav
. First, the rapidity of physical development of ou
tion systems in comparison with slower development o

d ability to produce goods without being able under
ibute and consume and enjoy them at a similar rate.

and concentration of money, and financial power,
er to serve the general good.

in which world peace efforts have been outstripped b

do about them?

ail are different of course for each of these proble
 to produce a sheaf of blue prints that will solve t
rength to do two things. One is to point these
atern on them so that our aroused national conscious
e them. Our national genius will be restless so lon
f the American people can see the needs of the prese
ie ways of the past and will adopt whatever new meth
 genius will save the day and they will need no furt
ind and the mass genius of the people have brought n
old outgrown ones before. One of the things tha
 to help hold the light.

"The other thing that I can do is to present one common denominator solution for all these problems I have raised and for almost all our other problems too. The solution is an informed and a thinking people functioning through a workable democracy that is free from the hysteria and passions of partisan politics, free from the traditions of a past that is no longer with us, unafraid to step on toes that may need to be stepped on for the national good, and patriotic enough to sacrifice in times of peace what others sacrifice in times of war. That is the kind of a patriotic democracy in which I place my confidence."

> "World Peace And Agriculture"
> Chester C. Davis
> Address: Institute of International Relations
> June 13, 1935.

Eliminate The Causes of War; Ryllis Alexander Goslin

"Among the causes of every war you will find, if you look closely, a strong economic reason. To return to Europe for a moment, consider the economic problems there. In an area one-third smaller than the United States there were, before the war, twenty different countries, each struggling for its own economic existence. To-day there are twenty six. Each one must have enough land for its people and produce or import enough goods to supply their needs.

"The war to end war failed to solve the economic problems that had been its root cause. For back of national jealousies and desire for power is always the pressure for more territory, greater resources increasing world markets.

"We have seen one of the chief causes of war to be economic. Every nation needs something which some other nation produces. But to-day goods are not ex-changed primarily for the purpose of supplying the needs of the people of various countries. Like the competition between rival merchants, nations are struggling with each other for control of existing markets. While governments are building tariff walls and fighting currency wars, three fourths of the people of the world do not have enough to eat. Yet modern science and modern machinery make it pos-sible to produce vast quantities of all of the things people need. At present we are not making full use of our knowledge or our machinery.

"If the needs of the people are to be supplied, it may be necessary to for-get national boundaries, as we have learned to forget state boundaries and make it possible for nations to exchange goods freely. This means the setting up of an in-telligent and fearless system of cooperation that would give every nation a chance to export the products it can best produce, and to import the goods it needs in return.

"International machinery, to be effective, must also consider problems of overpopulation, adjust political difficulties, revise treaties and establish a world system of law and order.

"Is such a world system possible? Thus far the nations have been unwilling to compromise or cooperate on vital issues which affect their national interests. As much as any other nation, the United States has refused to pay the price of real international cooperation. Some of our people say they do not like foreign

10797

nations and do not trust them. Others do not want to make the temporary sacrifices of reducing tariffs and canceling war debts.

"It was impossible in 1914 to go on 'doing business as usual' and still remain neutral. Therefore this year a strong anti war group in Congress presented a new neutrality program designed to keep our trade, our money and our citizens at home.

"No decision on the program had been reached by the third week in August when the situation between Italy and Ethiopia became acute. Congress was about to adjourn. There were urgent demands for action with regard to neutrality. Finally, a few days before Congress adjourned a compromise resolution was introduced and adopted.

"The compromise resolution ignores credits and loans and fails to recognize the importance of foodstuffs, cotton and other goods as war materials. It is designed merely to take care of the immediate crisis, and leave the way open for further discussion and the passage of permanent legislation at the next session. There will be many arguments for and against a permanent neutrality program. Above all, war profits would benefit all of us, directly or indirectly, as they did in 1915 and 1916. Business needs stimulation. More than ten million men are unemployed. A war would bring prosperity. It would open factories and create jobs. It would raise wages and increase profits for farmers, factory owners, shop keepers and investors. Would we--you and I--be able to resist war profits? To accept them means war.

"The new scientific age of power has bound all the nations of the world together. Our fate is tied up, whether we like it or not, with the fate of Germany, of Italy, of Russia, of Japan. As long as there is war anywhere in the world, we are in danger of being drawn into it, or of being hurt by it. It is imperative, therefore, that we join with other nations in an intelligent and determined effort to eliminate the causes of war. These causes are part of the warp and woof of our social and economic life. They arise out of the competitive struggle for material wealth and political p wer. It may be necessary to make fundamental changes in the social and economic structure before we can substitute international friendship for jealous nationalism, and cooperation for competition. It is not enough for us Americans to say, 'we don't like war.' We said that in 1914."

"War To-Morrow"
Pyllis Alexander Goslin
Headline Books, No. 1
The Foreign Policy Assoc.

Great Nations Are Nourished In War And Waste In Peace: John Ruskin

"It was very strange to me to discover this; and very dreadful--but I saw it to be quite an undeniable fact. The common notion that peace and the virtues of civil life flourished together, I found to be wholly untenable. Peace and the vices of civil life only flourish together. We talk of peace and learning, and of peace and plenty, and of peace and civilization; but I found that those were not the words which the Muse of History coupled together; that on her lips, the words

10797

were--peace and sensuality, peace and selfishness, peace and corruption, peace
and death. I found, in brief, that all great nations learned their truth of word
and strength of thought in war; that they were nourished in war and wasted in peace,
trained by war, and betrayed by peace;--in a word, that they were born in war and
expired in peace."

Lecture, "War"
John Ruskin

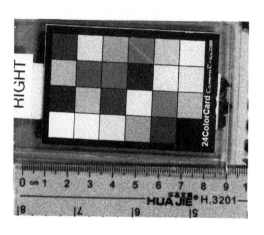

CPSIA information can be obtained
at www.ICGtesting.com
Printed in the USA
BVHW04*2044150918

527538BV00027B/512/P